Enjoy Every Day

DATE TODAY _____

PRIORITIES	TO DO	MEETINGS

NOTES

Enjoy Every Day

DATE TODAY _____

PRIORITIES	TO DO	MEETINGS

NOTES

Enjoy Every Day

DATE TODAY _____

PRIORITIES	TO DO	MEETINGS

NOTES

Enjoy Every Day

DATE TODAY

PRIORITIES	TO DO	MEETINGS

NOTES

Enjoy Every Day

DATE TODAY _____

PRIORITIES	TO DO	MEETINGS

NOTES

Enjoy Every Day

DATE TODAY _____

PRIORITIES	TO DO	MEETINGS

NOTES

Enjoy Every Day

DATE TODAY _____

PRIORITIES	TO DO	MEETINGS

NOTES

Enjoy Every Day

DATE TODAY _____

PRIORITIES	TO DO	MEETINGS

NOTES

Enjoy Every Day

DATE TODAY _____

PRIORITIES	TO DO	MEETINGS

NOTES

Enjoy Every Day

DATE TODAY _____

PRIORITIES	TO DO	MEETINGS

NOTES

Enjoy Every Day

DATE TODAY _____

PRIORITIES	TO DO	MEETINGS

NOTES

Enjoy Every Day

DATE TODAY

PRIORITIES	TO DO	MEETINGS

NOTES

Enjoy Every Day

DATE TODAY

PRIORITIES	TO DO	MEETINGS

NOTES

Enjoy Every Day

DATE TODAY _____

PRIORITIES	TO DO	MEETINGS

NOTES

Enjoy Every Day

DATE TODAY _____

PRIORITIES	TO DO	MEETINGS

NOTES

Enjoy Every Day

DATE TODAY _____

PRIORITIES	TO DO	MEETINGS

NOTES

Enjoy Every Day

DATE TODAY _____

PRIORITIES	TO DO	MEETINGS

NOTES

Enjoy Every Day

DATE TODAY _____

PRIORITIES	TO DO	MEETINGS

NOTES

Enjoy Every Day

DATE TODAY _____

PRIORITIES	TO DO	MEETINGS

NOTES

_____
_____
_____
_____
_____

Enjoy Every Day

DATE TODAY _____

PRIORITIES	TO DO	MEETINGS

NOTES

Enjoy Every Day

DATE TODAY _____

PRIORITIES	TO DO	MEETINGS

NOTES

Enjoy Every Day

DATE TODAY _____

PRIORITIES	TO DO	MEETINGS

NOTES

Enjoy Every Day

DATE TODAY _____

PRIORITIES	TO DO	MEETINGS

NOTES

Enjoy Every Day

DATE TODAY

PRIORITIES	TO DO	MEETINGS

NOTES

Enjoy Every Day

DATE TODAY _____

PRIORITIES	TO DO	MEETINGS

NOTES

Enjoy Every Day

DATE TODAY

PRIORITIES	TO DO	MEETINGS

NOTES

Enjoy Every Day

DATE TODAY

PRIORITIES	TO DO	MEETINGS

NOTES

Enjoy Every Day

DATE TODAY _____

PRIORITIES	TO DO	MEETINGS

NOTES

Enjoy Every Day

DATE TODAY _____

PRIORITIES	TO DO	MEETINGS

NOTES

Enjoy Every Day

DATE TODAY _____

PRIORITIES	TO DO	MEETINGS

NOTES

Enjoy Every Day

DATE TODAY _____

PRIORITIES	TO DO	MEETINGS

NOTES

Enjoy Every Day

DATE TODAY _____

PRIORITIES	TO DO	MEETINGS

NOTES

Enjoy Every Day

DATE TODAY _____

PRIORITIES	TO DO	MEETINGS

NOTES

Enjoy Every Day

DATE TODAY

PRIORITIES	TO DO	MEETINGS

NOTES

Enjoy Every Day

DATE TODAY _____

PRIORITIES	TO DO	MEETINGS

NOTES

Enjoy Every Day

DATE TODAY _____

PRIORITIES	TO DO	MEETINGS

NOTES

Enjoy Every Day

DATE TODAY _____

PRIORITIES	TO DO	MEETINGS

NOTES

Enjoy Every Day

DATE TODAY _____

PRIORITIES	TO DO	MEETINGS

NOTES

Enjoy Every Day

DATE TODAY _____

PRIORITIES	TO DO	MEETINGS

NOTES

Enjoy Every Day

DATE TODAY _____

PRIORITIES	TO DO	MEETINGS

NOTES

_____
_____
_____
_____
_____

Enjoy Every Day

DATE TODAY _____

PRIORITIES	TO DO	MEETINGS

NOTES

_____
_____
_____
_____
_____

Enjoy Every Day

DATE TODAY

PRIORITIES	TO DO	MEETINGS

NOTES

Enjoy Every Day

DATE TODAY _____

PRIORITIES	TO DO	MEETINGS

NOTES

Enjoy Every Day

DATE TODAY

PRIORITIES	TO DO	MEETINGS

NOTES

Enjoy Every Day

DATE TODAY _____

PRIORITIES	TO DO	MEETINGS

NOTES

Enjoy Every Day

DATE TODAY _____

PRIORITIES	TO DO	MEETINGS

NOTES

Enjoy Every Day

DATE TODAY _____

PRIORITIES	TO DO	MEETINGS

NOTES

Enjoy Every Day

DATE TODAY _____

PRIORITIES	TO DO	MEETINGS

NOTES

Enjoy Every Day

DATE TODAY _____

PRIORITIES	TO DO	MEETINGS

NOTES

Enjoy Every Day

DATE TODAY _____

PRIORITIES	TO DO	MEETINGS

NOTES

Enjoy Every Day

DATE TODAY

PRIORITIES	TO DO	MEETINGS

NOTES

Enjoy Every Day

DATE TODAY _____

PRIORITIES	TO DO	MEETINGS

NOTES

_____
_____
_____
_____
_____

Enjoy Every Day

DATE TODAY _____

PRIORITIES	TO DO	MEETINGS

NOTES

Enjoy Every Day

DATE TODAY _____

PRIORITIES	TO DO	MEETINGS

NOTES

Enjoy Every Day

DATE TODAY _____

PRIORITIES	TO DO	MEETINGS

NOTES

Enjoy Every Day

DATE TODAY _____

PRIORITIES	TO DO	MEETINGS

NOTES

Enjoy Every Day

DATE TODAY _____

PRIORITIES	TO DO	MEETINGS

NOTES

Enjoy Every Day

DATE TODAY _____

PRIORITIES	TO DO	MEETINGS

NOTES

Enjoy Every Day

DATE TODAY _____

PRIORITIES	TO DO	MEETINGS

NOTES

Enjoy Every Day

DATE TODAY _____

PRIORITIES	TO DO	MEETINGS

NOTES

Enjoy Every Day

DATE TODAY

PRIORITIES	TO DO	MEETINGS

NOTES

Enjoy Every Day

DATE TODAY _____

PRIORITIES	TO DO	MEETINGS

NOTES

_____
_____
_____
_____
_____

Enjoy Every Day

DATE TODAY _____

PRIORITIES	TO DO	MEETINGS

NOTES

Enjoy Every Day

DATE TODAY _____

PRIORITIES	TO DO	MEETINGS

NOTES

Enjoy Every Day

DATE TODAY

PRIORITIES	TO DO	MEETINGS

NOTES

Enjoy Every Day

DATE TODAY _____

PRIORITIES	TO DO	MEETINGS

NOTES

Enjoy Every Day

DATE TODAY _____

PRIORITIES	TO DO	MEETINGS

NOTES

Enjoy Every Day

DATE TODAY _____

PRIORITIES	TO DO	MEETINGS

NOTES

Enjoy Every Day

DATE TODAY _____

PRIORITIES	TO DO	MEETINGS

NOTES

Enjoy Every Day

DATE TODAY

PRIORITIES	TO DO	MEETINGS

NOTES

Enjoy Every Day

DATE TODAY _____

PRIORITIES	TO DO	MEETINGS

NOTES

Enjoy Every Day

DATE TODAY _____

PRIORITIES	TO DO	MEETINGS

NOTES

Enjoy Every Day

DATE TODAY _____

PRIORITIES	TO DO	MEETINGS

NOTES

Enjoy Every Day

DATE TODAY _____

PRIORITIES	TO DO	MEETINGS

NOTES

Enjoy Every Day

DATE TODAY _____

PRIORITIES	TO DO	MEETINGS

NOTES

Enjoy Every Day

DATE TODAY _____

PRIORITIES	TO DO	MEETINGS

NOTES

Enjoy Every Day

DATE TODAY

PRIORITIES	TO DO	MEETINGS

NOTES

Enjoy Every Day

DATE TODAY

PRIORITIES	TO DO	MEETINGS

NOTES

Enjoy Every Day

DATE TODAY _____

PRIORITIES	TO DO	MEETINGS

NOTES

Enjoy Every Day

DATE TODAY _____

PRIORITIES	TO DO	MEETINGS

NOTES

Enjoy Every Day

DATE TODAY _____

PRIORITIES	TO DO	MEETINGS

NOTES

Enjoy Every Day

DATE TODAY

PRIORITIES	TO DO	MEETINGS

NOTES

Enjoy Every Day

DATE TODAY _____

PRIORITIES	TO DO	MEETINGS

NOTES

Enjoy Every Day

DATE TODAY

PRIORITIES	TO DO	MEETINGS

NOTES

Enjoy Every Day

DATE TODAY

PRIORITIES	TO DO	MEETINGS

NOTES

Enjoy Every Day

DATE TODAY _____

PRIORITIES	TO DO	MEETINGS

NOTES

Enjoy Every Day

DATE TODAY _____

PRIORITIES	TO DO	MEETINGS

NOTES

Enjoy Every Day

DATE TODAY _____

PRIORITIES	TO DO	MEETINGS

NOTES

_____
_____
_____
_____
_____

Enjoy Every Day

DATE TODAY _____

PRIORITIES	TO DO	MEETINGS

NOTES

Enjoy Every Day

DATE TODAY

PRIORITIES	TO DO	MEETINGS

NOTES

Enjoy Every Day

DATE TODAY _____

PRIORITIES	TO DO	MEETINGS

NOTES

Enjoy Every Day

DATE TODAY _____

PRIORITIES	TO DO	MEETINGS

NOTES

Enjoy Every Day

DATE TODAY _____

PRIORITIES	TO DO	MEETINGS

NOTES

Enjoy Every Day

DATE TODAY _____

PRIORITIES	TO DO	MEETINGS

NOTES

Enjoy Every Day

DATE TODAY _____

PRIORITIES	TO DO	MEETINGS

NOTES

Enjoy Every Day

DATE TODAY _____

PRIORITIES	TO DO	MEETINGS

NOTES

Enjoy Every Day

DATE TODAY

PRIORITIES	TO DO	MEETINGS

NOTES

Enjoy Every Day

DATE TODAY _____

PRIORITIES	TO DO	MEETINGS

NOTES

Enjoy Every Day

DATE TODAY _____

PRIORITIES	TO DO	MEETINGS

NOTES

Enjoy Every Day

DATE TODAY _____

PRIORITIES	TO DO	MEETINGS

NOTES

Enjoy Every Day

DATE TODAY _____

PRIORITIES	TO DO	MEETINGS

NOTES

_____
_____
_____
_____
_____

Enjoy Every Day

DATE TODAY _____

PRIORITIES	TO DO	MEETINGS

NOTES

Enjoy Every Day

DATE TODAY _____

PRIORITIES	TO DO	MEETINGS

NOTES

Enjoy Every Day

DATE TODAY _____

PRIORITIES	TO DO	MEETINGS

NOTES

Enjoy Every Day

DATE TODAY _____

PRIORITIES	TO DO	MEETINGS

NOTES

Enjoy Every Day

DATE TODAY _____

PRIORITIES	TO DO	MEETINGS

NOTES

Enjoy Every Day

DATE TODAY _____

PRIORITIES	TO DO	MEETINGS

NOTES

Enjoy Every Day

DATE TODAY _____

PRIORITIES	TO DO	MEETINGS

NOTES

Enjoy Every Day

DATE TODAY _____

PRIORITIES	TO DO	MEETINGS

NOTES

Enjoy Every Day

DATE TODAY _____

PRIORITIES	TO DO	MEETINGS

NOTES

Enjoy Every Day

DATE TODAY _____

PRIORITIES	TO DO	MEETINGS

NOTES

_____
_____
_____
_____
_____

Enjoy Every Day

DATE TODAY _____

PRIORITIES	TO DO	MEETINGS

NOTES

Enjoy Every Day

DATE TODAY _____

PRIORITIES	TO DO	MEETINGS

NOTES

Enjoy Every Day

DATE TODAY _____

PRIORITIES	TO DO	MEETINGS

NOTES

Enjoy Every Day

DATE TODAY _____

PRIORITIES	TO DO	MEETINGS

NOTES

Enjoy Every Day

DATE TODAY _____

PRIORITIES	TO DO	MEETINGS

NOTES

Enjoy Every Day

DATE TODAY _____

PRIORITIES	TO DO	MEETINGS

NOTES

Enjoy Every Day

DATE TODAY _____

PRIORITIES	TO DO	MEETINGS

NOTES

Enjoy Every Day

DATE TODAY _____

PRIORITIES	TO DO	MEETINGS

NOTES

Enjoy Every Day

DATE TODAY _____

PRIORITIES	TO DO	MEETINGS

NOTES